CRIMEBUSTERS
TERRORISM

KATIE RODEN

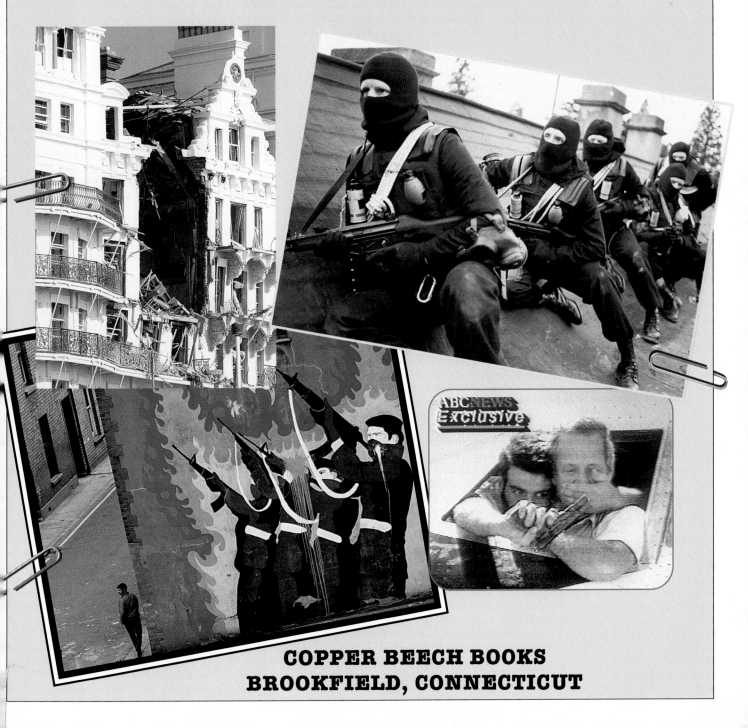

COPPER BEECH BOOKS
BROOKFIELD, CONNECTICUT

© Aladdin Books Ltd 1997
Designed and produced by
Aladdin Books Ltd
28 Percy Street
London W1P 0LD

*First published in
the United States in 1997 by*
Copper Beech Books,
an imprint of
The Millbrook Press
2 Old New Milford Road
Brookfield, Connecticut 06804

Editor Sarah Levete
Consultant
Richard Norton-Taylor, Special
Correspondent of The Guardian
Design
David West
Children's Book Design
Designer
Flick Killerby
Picture Research
Brooks Krikler Research

Printed in Belgium
All rights reserved

Picture credits *(t-top, m-middle,
b-bottom, r-right, l-left)*
*Cover t & m, 2tl & bl, 4, 4-5, 5 all, 6br,
6-7, 8b, 9 both, 10 both, 11 all, 12m &
b, 13t & b, 14b, 15 all, 16 both, 17t &
b, 18m & b, 19mr,20 tr & b, 21 all, 22
both, 23m & b, 24b, 24-25, 25t & m,
26br, 27t, 29b, 30 both & 31bl: Frank
Spooner Pictures; cover b, 14t, 18t, 20tl,
26t, 28 & 29m: Roger Vlitos; 2tr, 14-15
& 19ml: Solution Pictures; 2br & 13m:
courtesy ABC News; 6bl & 7 all:
Hulton Getty Collection; 8t, 12t, 19b,
22-23, 24t, 27b, 29tl & tr: Science
Photo Library; 8m, 26bl, 31t, m & br:
Rex Features; 19t & 25b: Trip Pictures.*

CONTENTS

INTRODUCTION

"A Terrible Threat"

Terrorism is the use of violence and threats to cause fear and terror. These criminal acts are most often committed in support of a political or social cause. Terrorists believe that these methods are the only way to gain publicity for their cause and to bring about social or political change.

Throughout history, people have used terror to achieve their own ends. However, technological advances have made the modern world more vulnerable to the threat of terrorism. Built-up areas where we live and work and busy international travel routes are easy targets for terrorist attacks against the entire population.

Terrorist acts may be aimed at individuals or organizations directly opposed to the terrorists' cause, but they often injure and kill innocent civilians. Whatever the motive for such attacks, from religion to politics, their aim is the same – to show that terrorists are powerful and dangerous.

This book looks at the methods used by police forces, anti-terrorist squads, forensic scientists, and bomb disposal teams worldwide to combat terrorism. It examines the ways in which the authorities try to prevent terrorist incidents and to track down the individuals responsible for such crimes.

CASE STUDY

FROM TIP-OFF TO DISCOVERY
In September 1996, a massive security operation led to the seizure of a huge explosives and arms cache (hidden store). Possibly tipped off by an informer (see page 20), two trucks were tracked from Ireland to Scotland, and finally to London, where IRA terrorists (see page 4) had rented a secure steel vault to store their weapons. Anti-terrorist branches and over 10 police forces were involved in the operation.

Unlike other violent criminals, terrorists create terror and carry out attacks on civilians in support of a specific cause, often political or religious. They may use violence to establish religious dominance within an area, or to achieve political independence from a country, as ETA (the Homeland and Liberty Movement) does (*see page 11*). However, one person's "terrorist" may be another person's "freedom fighter." For example, some people may approve of the use of violence to liberate a group from a harsh regime; to others, who do not sympathize with that cause, the violence is criminal, and is the action of terrorists.

CASE STUDY

THE CHECHEN CRISIS
In 1995, the Russian capital, Moscow, saw its first major terrorist incidents – bombs on the buses and the Metro. These were probably planted by terrorists from the province of Chechnya (*above*). The Chechens were fighting for independence from Russia, which at first, Boris Yeltsin, the Russian president refused.

The Politics of Fear
Some terrorist groups aim to get rid of governments that oppose their ideas. They use violence to protest against things which they feel are wrong. Founded in 1919, the IRA (Irish Republican Army, *right*) has used terrorism to try to achieve a United Ireland, politically independent from the United Kingdom.

Violent incidents may also be the work of gangs such as the Japanese Yakusa, shown here protesting against laws to limit their power.

FIGHTING FOR A CAUSE

Religion is a major motive for terrorist attacks, as some extreme religious groups try to establish their dominance over other religious groups through violence. Such groups often claim that they have a "right" to a particular area of land. It is also known as nationalism when a particular ethnic or religious group lays claim to a country or area.

The assassination of Israel's Jewish president, Yitzhak Rabin, in 1995 (*left*), was carried out in the name of a religious cause. He was shot by a Jewish extremist who did not agree with Rabin's policy of making peace with Palestinians, who are mostly Muslim Arabs, not Jewish.

CASE STUDY
Some terrorist groups are made up of extreme groups, often white racists, who believe that their race is better than anybody else's. The U.S. "militias" (*above*) want to ban people from other races or countries from living in "their" area, and want independence from the federal government.

It was 1:30 A.M. as the young policewoman gasped as the line went dead. She had just received the following message: "This is Alpha Ten, I repeat, code Alpha Ten. At approximately 5:30 A.M. today, an explosive device will be detonated in the city center." She quickly called the sergeant, who realized at once that this was no hoax – it was a bomb warning. Alpha Ten was the code used by an organization known as the TMS. Instantly, the station sprang into life. All units were ordered to the city center with instructions to evacuate the streets and nearby buildings. Bomb squads and disposal teams were also summoned to the area.

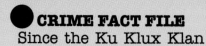

CRIME FACT FILE
Since the Ku Klux Klan *(below)* terrorized African-Americans after the Civil War (1861-1865), there has been a frightening rise in such racist groups. Adolf Hitler, the Nazi dictator from 1933-1945, was responsible for the murder of millions of Jewish people. Today, some terrorist groups are emerging who are prepared to use violence in a similar way.

BEGINNINGS

Terrorism is not simply a twentieth-century phenomenon. People have fought against unpopular regimes or governments with violence since ancient times. The word "terrorism" first appeared in records of the French Revolution (1789-1799), when some of the revolutionaries who seized power ruled with violence. Perhaps the world's most famous early terrorists were Guy Fawkes (1570-1606) and the gunpowder plotters *(left)*. In an example of religious terrorism, the gang plotted to assassinate the Protestant King James I (VI of Scotland), and his Parliament, so that a Catholic ruler could replace him. However, they were caught before they could set off the barrels of gunpowder, and were condemned to death.

THE RISE OF TERROR

Terrorist tactics have been used in many countries by groups of anarchists, such as Action Directe in France *(see page 31).* Anarchists are people who believe that any form of rule or government is wrong. They use violence to try and overthrow governments. Anarchist groups also played a part in the Spanish Civil War (1936-1939, *right).*

A wave of "political" terrorism began in the 1960s. This was carried out by groups such as the Red Brigades in Italy and the Red Army Faction in former West Germany, who wanted to destroy and replace the political system in their countries.

Other modern terrorist movements have been inspired by the demands of ethnic minorities for political independence or domination in an area.

A MODERN TERROR

In the 1930s, Germany, Italy, and the former Soviet Union were dominated by dictators. Hitler in Germany, Mussolini in Italy, and Stalin in the former Soviet Union *(below)* used terrorist methods of violence and threats to maintain their rule. They were responsible for the deaths of millions of citizens.

More recently, some governments have used terrorist tactics to ensure that they stifle any opposition. For instance, it is known that such "state" terrorism has been adopted by Libya, Iran and Iraq, which have authorized the assassinations of political opponents.

THE BAADER-MEINHOF GANG

While trying to catch six of the world's most wanted terrorists, on May 4, 1979, German police shot dead Elisabeth von Dyck *(below)*, a supposed member of the notorious Baader-Meinhof gang. The former West German Baader-Meinhof gang was a terrorist group of young people who wanted to change the system of the country. Trained by the PLO *(see page 11)* in Lebanon, they carried out various sieges and kidnappings in the early 1970s. The German anti-terrorist squad, the GSG-9, was set up in response to their terrorist activities.

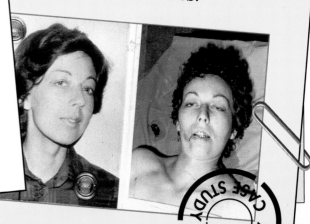

The Bombing

Within half an hour, the area was sealed off. Hundreds of frightened civilians stood by the cordon while the bomb squad painstakingly searched stores, cars, buses, and garbage bins... but found nothing. Minutes before 5:30 all the buildings had been

evacuated and the bomb disposal team had withdrawn to a safe distance. At precisely 5:30, a huge bomb exploded. Windows shattered, showering the police with fragments of glass. The area was devastated – offices, stores, and some homes had been completely destroyed.

Hijacking

This is a high-profile form of terrorism which involves seizing a vehicle, such as an airplane or ship, by force or the threat of force. It gives the terrorists time to make their demands and ideas known.

Some hijackers hold prisoners for ransom, demanding money or action from a government. Others may demand that a plane or ship be diverted to take them to another country. The picture above shows three of the 365 people held on a plane for over 16 hours in 1995 by a Japanese hijacker, Fumi Kutsumi. In fact, he was armed with only a screwdriver.

Bombing

From small, homemade bombs like the one that disrupted the 1996 Olympic Games (see page 21) to huge devices that fill whole trucks, bombing is a devastating form of terrorism, and one which is favored by most terrorists. Some groups give coded warnings before a bomb is due to explode; others do not, often causing a massive loss of life and injury (below).

Guerrilla Warfare

Guerrillas (the word means "little war" in Spanish) are groups of roving fighters who use small-scale terrorist attacks to further their cause. Many operate in small bands in rural areas. Today, guerrilla warfare is used against governments. Guerrillas do not deliberately target civilians; instead, their aim is to persuade the people to join their fight.

Case Study

LOCKERBIE

On December 21, 1988, a Pan Am Boeing 747 jet crashed down onto the Scottish town of Lockerbie, killing all 259 people on board and 11 people from the town. As the wreckage was examined (below), it was revealed that U.S. embassies had been warned of a terrorist attack on a Pan Am flight. The cause of the disaster was indeed a bomb. The United States and England have formally accused two Libyan intelligence officers of planting the bomb. However, the Libyan government refuses to extradite the suspects (see page 17).

Hostage-taking

Like hijacking, hostage-taking is another way for terrorists to put pressure on the authorities to agree to their demands. Many terrorists threaten their hostages with death or injury if their needs are not met. In extreme cases they will kill or injure their victims one by one, to show the authorities that they are serious.

The Iranian Embassy siege (above) in London, 1980, began with the death of a policewoman and ended with the death of two out of five of the terrorists. The terrorists were Arab extremists intent on gaining political recognition for the Iranian province of Khuzistan. Many people now believe that the operation could have been resolved more peaceably.

As soon as the warning had been received, ambulance and fire crews had been summoned to the scene. They now combed the wreckage for bodies or survivors of the blast. But thanks to the quick action of the police, nobody was seriously hurt. A forensic squad was dispatched to the scene. They began searching the area and identified the probable source of the bomb – an almost unrecognizable car. What remained of the vehicle was taken away for scientific examination. Officers continued to look for other clues which would help them identify the bomber. Any fragments of evidence were sent to the forensic laboratory for analysis.

CRIME FACT FILE
Many established terrorist groups, such as the IRA, are well organized, with leaders whose orders the members obey. Today, there is an increase in the number of terrorists working alone, and not for any group. For instance, in 1993, a lone terrorist, Sheik Omar Abdel Rahman, carried out the bombing of the World Trade Center, in New York City.

MAFIA

One of the most feared groups in the world is the Mafia, a widespread organization based on the fourteenth-century Mafia of Sicily. The largest element is the U.S. Mafia, although various groups are prominent in Italy. The Mafia makes money and wields power through organized crime such as drug trafficking and money laundering. Its members are prepared to use terrorism against those who threaten their power. Judges who prosecute Mafia members, police officers who investigate their activities, and anyone who informs against them may be victims of car bombings or assassinations. When their members are tried, they are kept behind bars, and those prosecuting them are often hidden by screens for protection.

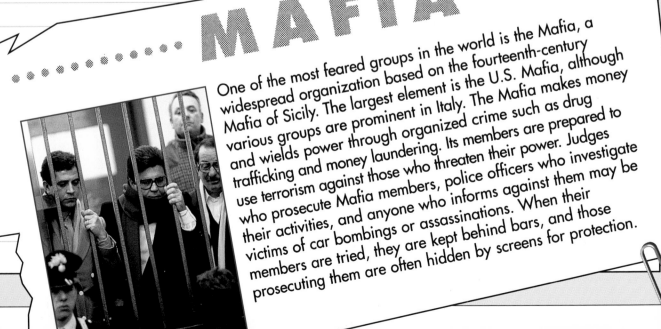

ETA

CRIME FACT FILE

Formed in 1988, Hamas (Islamic Resistance Movement, *below*) are fighting for an independent Palestinian state under Islamic law. Hamas reject any peace settlement in the troubled Middle East and call for the destruction of Israel. In October 1994, a Hamas suicide bomber (*see page 22*) killed 21 civilians and injured 45 others on a bus in Tel Aviv, Israel. In addition to other extreme Islamic terrorist groups, such as Hizbollah (*see page 30*), and Islamic Jihad, there is a disturbing new terrorist threat from extreme Islamic groups who have no formal organization or leadership.

Formed in 1959, the Homeland and Liberty Movement (ETA, *above*) is dedicated to achieving independence for the Basque region of northwestern Spain. Assassinations and murders are the hallmarks of the group: In July 1986, it murdered nine members of the Civil Guard by blowing up the bus in which they were traveling.

More recently, ETA has carried out regular "beach bomb" campaigns during the summer months, to strike at Spain's important tourist industry. These bombs, planted along the popular Mediterranean coast, are intended to frighten rather than injure. However, a bomb placed in a garbage bin at Reus Airport near Barcelona went off early when it was discovered by a cleaner. The bomb injured 35 people.

CASE STUDY

THE PLO

The Palestine Liberation Organization (PLO) was formed in 1964 to fight for the rights of Palestinian people to a homeland. Accused of being a terrorist group, the PLO claimed it was a national liberation movement. Its chairman, Yasser Arafat (*right*), is now involved in efforts to establish peace with Palestine's neighbor, Israel, but some extreme PLO members have left to form terrorist organizations.

Does Terrorism Work?
Some groups previously described as terrorist groups, such as the PLO (*see left*) and the ANC (African National Congress), have become respected political parties. Did their violence win them recognition, or was it the validity of their cause?

The Bombing

One week later, much of the wreckage had been cleared from the area; life in the city was returning to normal. But for the police, the investigation had only just begun. All the fragments had been analyzed at the forensic laboratory and many had been found to contain traces of Semtex explosive. This was a favorite weapon of the terrorist organization TMS – and their code had been used in the tip-off. The bomber was likely to have been one of their members. Soon more news came from the lab. Samples of skin, fibers, and hair had been found on the car used by the bomber.

Cooperation

The major terrorist organizations do not operate in isolation. They sometimes have strong links to other groups with similar aims in other countries. These links can be very important in coordinating terrorist activities. The groups supply each other with weapons and fake passports (such as these seized by the police, *above*), and help each other's members to escape from prison.

Such networks mean that the groups can send their members quickly and securely around the world. This is important to terrorist groups because they often have to move from one country to another, to avoid capture by the anti-terrorist organizations.

Training

Terrorists often use the media (TV, radio, and newspapers) to make their demands or to bring public attention to their cause. Many people think that terrorists should not be allowed to use the media in this way.

Dramatic pictures of terrorists' victims may be beamed around the world to try and pressure governments into agreeing to their demands. The picture *(left)* shows a

television interview with a hijacker at Beirut Airport, 1985, while the pilot, John Testrake, is held at gunpoint.

Recently, the relatives of hostages have begun high-profile media campaigns themselves to encourage terrorists to release their victims. The picture above shows the supporters of hostages taken by Kashmiri terrorists in India *(see page 31)*, trying to secure their release.

Different terrorist groups also train each other's members. This means that the training is kept secret from their native country's authorities. The terrorists' training is often similar to that of a country's special military forces, combining weaponry knowledge and survival skills *(left)*. Reports of terrorist activity in the media have enabled groups to copy each other's methods. The kidnapping of a U.S. ambassador in Brazil, in 1969, which secured the release of convicted terrorists from Brazilian jails, was copied by many groups worldwide.

Case Study

THE UNABOMBER

Theodore J. Kaczynski, currently in prison in Sacramento, California, is thought to be the lone terrorist known as the Unabomber. For 17 years, the Unabomber sent letter bombs to people working in education and technology, killing three people and injuring 28. He published a

thousand-word "manifesto" in two national newspapers, in which he aired his grievances.

The Weakness

The growth of communication networks has given terrorist groups more skills and coordination, but it also means that they are more vulnerable to discovery. Anti-terrorist organizations hope that this weakness will help them to gain important details about the activities of the world's terrorists.

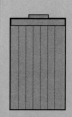

While the forensics team began to analyze the traces of evidence from the car, the police were busy chasing their contacts for any leads to help them catch the bomber. Via Interpol (the International Criminal Police Organization), they informed police forces around the world about the investigation. Immediately, French police sources passed on details they had received from an anonymous informer, giving a list of known activists within the TMS. They knew that one of these people, Andy Dawson, was in mainland Britiain.

ANTI-TERRORIST SQUADS

Around the world there are many anti-terrorist squads to help combat the increasing threat of terrorism. These anti-terrorist groups include:

- special units in the FBI (Federal Bureau of Investigation, *left*);
- the German GSG-9, a specialist police unit;
- branches of the Italian Carabinieri, or police;
- the military British SAS (Special Air Squadron) and the terrorist branch of Scotland Yard (British police force);
- the Israeli Paras, a military airborne unit;
- the French GIGN (Groupe d'Intervention Gendarmerie Nationale), made up of officers from the Gendamerie Nationale, or police force.

CRIME FACT FILE

When protecting dignitaries (important people), special officers *(below)* must be alert at all times. If the person is attacked, they must protect him or her at all costs, whatever the dangers they themselves might be facing.

WACO

In 1993, more than 80 members of a religious cult died on a ranch at Waco, Texas. Many of them had been held hostage there for 51 weeks by their leader, David Koresh. Finally, the FBI ambushed and set fire to the ranch *(left)*. The FBI was criticized for taking direct action, showing how sensitive hostage situations can be.

A SKILLED JOB

All anti-terrorist officers must undergo a long, difficult, and highly specialized period of training. They learn how to use a variety of weapons and equipment, and are taught unarmed combat and the difficult task of negotiating with hostage-takers. Each country has its own methods of training. For example, officers in Algeria are taught in the Ninja tradition *(left)*. The Ninjas, a Japanese clan operating from the 12th to the 14th centuries, were trained to be both stealthy and deadly.

THE DUTIES

To combat the growing number of terrorist attacks, anti-terrorist squads focus on three main areas in their work. "Intelligence" is crucial in helping the authorities to stay one step ahead of the terrorists, and to track down the people who carry out any terrorist crimes *(see page 20)*. Protecting important people *(left)* who may be targets for terrorist attacks is another way of trying to prevent any incidents. Anti-terrorist squads also intervene in hostage situations, working closely with the police.

Protecting the Innocent

Unless terrorist incidents are handled carefully, innocent people can lose their lives or freedom. Anti-terrorist organizations and police forces have sometimes used illegal and excessive methods to secure the capture and conviction of terrorists. In the United Kingdom, several IRA convictions have been overruled due to the discovery of the unlawful tactics used by the police.

15

The Bombing

As soon as the call had come through, Dawson's records were called up from the national computer database. These showed suspected links with various extreme terrorist organizations, most notably the TMS. The TMS was well known as a strict right-wing terrorist group. They had already killed four people this year, in the name of their cause.

 Although the police had no hard evidence, Dawson was definitely a prime suspect. Undercover officers were sent to locate him, with instructions not to raise his suspicions. They soon found him living in the city.

Arrests

Differing laws worldwide can make tracking and catching terrorists complicated. If a person or group is arrested in one country (*below*), the treatment they receive may not be the same as that in another country. When someone is arrested when they are abroad, difficult questions are raised. Should he or she be treated by the law of that country, or be sent back to face punishment at home?

Go to Jail

The power of the terrorist organizations, and the fact that different groups may help each other's members to escape, mean that terrorist suspects are usually held in top-security jails and are often isolated from other prisoners.

 People who have helped to imprison them are usually protected because revenge killings are common, especially by large, well-organized groups such as the IRA or the Shining Path of Peru (*see page 30*). Abimael Guzman, the leader of the Shining Path, is seen here in jail (*right*).

Border Controls

Each country must patrol and check its borders, to look for terrorists and any illegal equipment moving from country to country. Extra care is taken in areas where major terrorist groups are known to be active. Easing the border regulations between different countries, such as those within the European Community, and the increasing movement of people between different countries, present anti-terrorist organizations and the police with huge problems.

Extradition

Extradition is the surrender of a person by one country to another to stand trial for crimes alleged to have been committed in that country. It is still a major problem for anti-terrorist

organizations. Extradition laws vary from country to country: While some will extradite any suspects, other countries refuse to extradite their own citizens or people married to their own citizens. The host country may hold similar views to the terrorist or may consider him or her only to be politically active, not criminal. This means that many terrorists now live in countries from which they cannot be taken for trial: In this way they can evade the law.

A United Fight

Governments can make it hard for terrorists to operate across frontiers or to be supported in another country. In 1996, the British proposed an amendment to a United Nations rule. This would stop a person involved in terrorism from being given asylum or refuge in another country.

Case study

In September 1996, Ramzi Ahmed Yousef was found guilty of planning to blow up 12 airliners bound for the U.S. He had previously evaded border controls by using 40 aliases (false identities), with papers to support each one. When he was arrested in Pakistan, he was found to have three passports.

The Bombing

The police hoped that by tracking Dawson, they would be led to other members of the group and perhaps to secret weapons or even the plans of the TMS. Two officers followed every move he made outside his house. Tiny surveillance cameras were pushed through the walls to watch his movements indoors and his phone calls were traced. Several numbers of suspected TMS members appeared. The police decided that they had enough information to question Dawson. The squad dispatched to bring the suspect in found him watching television. Although uncooperative, Dawson was persuaded to accompany them to the police station for questioning.

Crime Fact File

Many people believe that worldwide security will be improved when countries no longer offer support to terrorist groups. Colonel Muammar El-Qaddafi of Libya is known to have offered terrorists refuge and arms. In order to persuade countries to stop backing terrorists, other governments may impose economic sanctions (cutting off trade links) on them. But for political or historical reasons, some governments may be reluctant to become involved in action over terrorist activity that has affected another country.

Safe Cities

Large towns and cities are often terrorist targets because they are built-up, busy areas where majo damage can be caused. For ove 20 years, London has been the target of IRA bombs. After bomb struck at the heart of London's business area, the "City," securit was stepped up. There are now cordons around the area. Most vehicles are not allowed in the security area; those permitted are checked and the drivers are questioned (left).

With the worldwide increase of terrorist attacks, security at the world's airports is now rigorous, but not yet tight enough to prevent all incidents. All bags are X-rayed and any suspect passengers are tracked carefully. Sniffer dogs, trained to find explosives and drugs, examine luggage behind the scenes, and all aircraft are checked before take-off. However, some airport authorities have been reluctant to spend vast amounts of money on sophisticated scanning machines which could detect even plastic explosives and weapons, such as the Glock gun *(below right)* and Semtex *(below)*. Some security measures would be too time-consuming – such as passengers identifying their luggage before they board the aircraft, ensuring that every item on the plane belongs to someone who is on the flight.

Airport X-ray machines detect guns and other weapons.

Glock

The detection of weapons is an important feature of combating terrorism. The Glock *(below)* is a popular semi-automatic gun used by the Austrian police and some special forces. However, it is also favored by terrorists.

Case Study

SEMTEX

Plastic explosives such as Semtex (the white substance, *left*) are important tools in terrorist campaigns. They are small, light, and odorless. They are extremely powerful. About two pounds of Semtex, built into a cassette recorder, was enough to bring down the airplane in the Lockerbie disaster *(see page 9)*.

Although the Glock's barrel is made of steel and the gun uses metal-cased ammunition, both of which sophisticated X-ray machines could detect, its plastic frame, trigger, and magazine make it difficult for current airport security X rays to pick up.

Dawson sullenly climbed into the police car, which sped away to a high-security police station. Here his details and fingerprints were taken. In the interview room, Dawson was questioned about his connections with the TMS and the recent city center bombing. Dawson repeatedly denied his involvement. But the police pressed on, although they had to presume that Dawson was innocent until they knew otherwise. While the interview continued, officers searched Dawson's house and car for anything that might link him to the crime. After several hours, without finding anything significant, they decided to call off the search.

INTELLIGENCE WORK

Anti-terrorist organizations may use undercover work to help them track suspects. This work involves the use of informers and intelligence work by undercover officers to infiltrate (secretly enter) terrorist groups. Officers also investigate the bank accounts of suspects to see if large amounts of money have been spent, which could be used to buy arms or other equipment. Terrorists often make use of international differences in banking laws to hide their transactions and to safeguard their money *(below)*.

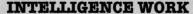

The Group of Seven

Known as G7, this group *(right)* includes the leaders of the world's most powerful industrialized countries. In 1996, together with Russia, the group agreed on 25 measures to fight terrorism. These included intelligence-sharing, tougher border controls, and action against fundraising by terrorists.

CASE STUDY CASE STUDY

ARMS SMUGGLING

Deprived of their weapons, terrorists would no longer pose a threat. However, arms dealing is a major world industry which terrorists exploit by illegal trading in guns, explosives, and other weapons. Arms dealers have found ways of avoiding the restrictions imposed on them by various countries. As a result, terrorists can buy weapons from other terrorist groups worldwide. Some weapons are supplied by states who support terrorism in countries to which they are opposed. Terrorists take elaborate steps to hide weapons in huge underground bunkers or other concealed places, like the arms cache shown right, in Washington, D.C.

SMALL BUT DEADLY

Despite tight security, terrorists still find ways of smuggling explosives onto planes and boats. The use of plastic explosives (see page 19)
means that bombs can now be very small and easily concealed in ordinary items. These can be packed into a suitcase

and hidden among other luggage waiting to be put aboard the vehicle. The pack of cigarettes, bag of candy, and book shown here all contain bombs – it is no wonder that devices like these are very hard to detect.

CASE STUDY
In 1996, the IRA planted two bombs in an army barracks in Northern Ireland. A security camera which may have helped police to identify and trace the terrorists was not working at the time.

At the Olympic Games in Atlanta, 1996, extensive security measures were taken. 30,000 law-enforcement officers, 11,000 National Guardsmen, more than 500 Delta Force and SEAL-Team 6 Commandos, officers from the Army's 160th Special Operations Aviation Regiment, specially trained U.S. Army Rangers, and other officers were at the Games to detect any suspicious activity or individuals in the crowds.

However, this massive security operation failed to prevent the explosion of a bomb.

Giving a final look around Dawson's backyard, in frustration an officer kicked a stone beside the garden shed. "What a waste of time," he thought. Then he looked again and saw that he had dislodged a pile of stones covering some wooden boards. Two officers with shovels joined the search. The wooden boards revealed a trap door leading to a bunker, probably an old air-raid shelter. This time they had hit the jackpot – inside the bunker, concealed in boxes, were arms and what looked like materials for a bomb factory.

One very good way of checking for smuggled weapons or materials used to make explosives is body searches. However, this is expensive. In just three years, body searches cost almost $200 million. More efficient methods are being developed.

DYING FOR THE CAUSE.

Among terrorism's most terrifying supporters are suicide bombers, often associated with extreme religious organizations. The bombers, usually driving explosives-packed vehicles or hiding a bomb under their clothes, are used by terrorist groups to take devices into areas where the most havoc can be caused, such as busy streets or buildings. Extreme Islamic groups (see page 30), inspired by the promise that martyrs earn a privileged place in heaven, have used bombers of only 15 years old whose video-taped messages were played on Lebanese television after their deaths. People who hold such extreme beliefs are very difficult for the authorities to trace or stop. The picture above shows the devastation caused by a bombing in Jerusalem.

THE POWER OF THE BOMB

Bombs cause widespread damage, killing or injuring anyone who happens to be within the force of the bomb's blast.

Many terrorist bombs are "homemade," using materials such as gelignite and agricultural fertilizer as blasting powders, which are packed with nails and screws. The bomb which destroyed the Oklahoma Federal Building, in 1995 (below) was made up of 5,000 pounds of homemade explosives.

Despite the simplicity of such bombs, they can be fitted with timers which allow the bombers to plant a device or detonator (below left) some time before they want it to explode. This makes protecting prime targets like places where politicians will stay very difficult – how many weeks in advance can a site be checked for bombs? Sometimes, devices explode early. In 1996, an IRA bomber died when a device he was carrying exploded on a bus in London.

A police robot handles a bomb by remote control.

CASE STUDY

THE BRIGHTON BOMB

On October 12, 1984, an IRA bomb destroyed the Grand Hotel, Brighton, England, killing four people and wounding over 30. It was intended to be the IRA's most dramatic move yet – most of the leaders of the British Conservative government were staying in the hotel. Using a long-delay timer, the bomb had been planted some weeks in advance.

At the police station, Dawson was about to be released. There did not seem to be enough evidence to hold him. An urgent call came just in time, with news of the arms cache and homemade bomb factory. Dawson was held back for more questioning. At the house, officers took Dawson's clothes and the contents of the bunker to the laboratory. The forensic team got to work once again. Samples of plastic explosives matched exactly the type of explosive used in the bombing. Guns were tested to see if bullets fired from them matched those fired in other terrorist incidents.

WARNINGS AND CODES

Many of the larger terrorist organizations have established a system of codes which allows them to warn the police that a bomb is due to go off. This enables the police to clear the area and ensure that as many civilians as possible are saved. Some groups feel that the public will be more sympathetic to them if their actions do not involve huge losses of life. Warnings are often given in the form of passwords, which tell the police that the message is not a hoax.

DETONATION

If a suspect package is found, experts are usually sent in to detonate (explode) it, whether or not it is known to be a bomb. These actions are carefully controlled so little damage is caused to the surrounding area. Some police forces have special robots that can handle devices by remote control, to enable officers to keep clear of the bomb.
Explosives can remain live for many years – even today bomb experts (*right*) are still called out to perform controlled explosions of unexploded bombs from World War II (1939-1945).

SNIFFER DOGS
Despite all the hi-tech methods of detection available today, one of the most effective ways of finding hidden substances is by using sniffer dogs. These specially trained animals are used at airports, ports, and national borders to sniff out explosives and drugs. However, more "odorless" explosives such as Semtex (*see page 19*) make their task more difficult. Sniffer dogs are also able to find survivors or bodies trapped in the wreckage at bomb sites (or at the scene of natural disasters). They may also be used in the hunt for buried human remains.

SEARCHES

Searches for explosives and weapons can be carried out in many different ways. As well as using X rays at ports and airports, officers use mirrors and heat-sensitive devices to check the undersides of suspect vehicles. If a bomb warning is received, they carry out a detailed, careful check of the area in which the explosive is thought to be. All buildings, vehicles, unattended bags, garbage bins and anywhere else that a bomb could be hidden are checked. Even if no bomb is found, the search itself disrupts public life: Traffic is held up, roads are closed, and businesses are affected. Booby traps (devices that are disguised to look harmless) are often used by terrorist groups. They make the job of searching for bombs even more dangerous.

Searches are now routine at ports or at border crossings (see page 19).

The Legacy of Terrorism
Have you ever stepped off a plane and been alarmed to see armed police and armored cars waiting on the runway?

Terrorism has become a fact of life for the modern world. Although we are used to hearing about terrorist incidents, we never stop being appalled at the death and destruction they cause.

The scientists matched a fiber, found in the wreckage of the car in which the bomb had been planted, with threads from one of Dawson's sweaters taken from his house. Lists of potential TMS targets and timetables of campaigns found in the bunker provided more evidence. Dawson admitted that he had planted the bomb; but he would not name anyone else. The police suspected that he had not been told the names of the TMS's leaders so that they could escape arrest. There was a long way to go before the TMS could be stopped.

....TESTING....

Modern forensic techniques allow scientists to analyze almost every substance. Fibers, hairs, skin fragments, and minute

specks of paint can be seen and matched under powerful electron microscopes, while even the tiniest drop of blood or any other body part can now give scientists a DNA match. DNA contains genes, which give each of us our unique characteristics. It can be broken down into a chart, so samples from a crime scene can be matched with those of a suspect. In investigations such as a bombing, this can be very important – it can confirm if a suspect was not at the crime scene, as well as if he or she was there.

CRIME FACT FILE
Terrorist groups do not always admit to carrying out a terrorist act. This can make governments and people feel vulnerable; it is as if the terrorists hold the power. Only forensic evidence, found as the result of searches (below) can confirm the cause of an explosion. For instance, investigators are still looking for evidence to determine the reason why TWA Flight 800 fell into the sea in July 1996, killing all 230 people aboard.

THE GUILDFORD 4

In 1974, Gerald Conlon (*left*), Paul Hill, Patrick Armstrong, and Carole Richardson were imprisoned as IRA terrorists who had blown up a pub in Guildford, England. All four claimed they were innocent. A 14-year campaign led to the discovery that much of the evidence had been made up by the police. The appeal heard that substances found on rubber gloves of one of Conlon's relatives, described at the trial as being components of a homemade bomb, could have come from ordinary household substances. Their convictions were quashed in 1989.

CASE STUDY CASE STUDY

WAS IT A BOMB?

As soon as an explosion is reported, forensic scientists rush to the scene to search for clues as to whether it was caused by accident (such as a gas leak) or by a terrorist attack. They examine the debris (wreckage) carefully. The pattern of the explosion can tell them whether it was caused by gas, which pushes debris straight out from the center of the blast. A bomb produces a blast of great force from a single point which gradually dies away. The depth to which fragments of debris have been buried in walls by the force of a blast can be measured to figure out the speed at which they traveled: Above 3,300 feet per second usually indicates a bomb blast. Once this has been decided, the debris is examined for possible pieces of the bomb. Even the tiniest fragment is sent to the laboratory for examination. The type of timer used in the bomb (*see below*) can indicate when it was planted.

Forensic scientists are also able to identify the specific gun from which a bullet may have been fired (*below*). Their evidence often provides the most exact proof of a crime.

How to Detect a Bomb Blast

An explosion may occur for several reasons. There are various ways of discovering if it was caused by a bomb:

1. The pattern of the debris (*see above*).
2. Fragments of printed circuit board can indicate an electronic timer which can be programmed months in advance.
3. Fragments of a clock or watch, which may suggest a clockwork timer — this can only be set a short time in advance.
4. Burning or melting on items. This suggests that they were parts of the bomb and were singed during the explosion.

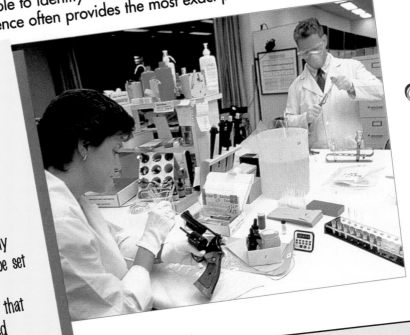

THE TRIAL

At Dawson's trial, security was tight as officers feared that the TMS might try to force the release of their bomber. The police had been careful to ensure that every official procedure had been followed to the letter, so that Dawson could not escape on a legal technicality.

1 Telephone records clearly established Dawson as actively in contact with the TMS.

2 Threads from one of Dawson's sweaters matched those found in the car which had been carrying the bomb.

3 A substantial arms cache had been discovered in Dawson's yard.

4 Bomb-making equipment had been discovered in Dawson's yard.

5 Fingerprints on the arms and bomb-making equipment matched those of Dawson exactly.

6 Documents and papers recovered at Dawson's house suggested that he was involved in a major terrorist campaign which was targeting politicians and civilians alike.

The jury found Dawson guilty. Dawson continued to refuse to give the police any names, contacts, or addresses. He was convicted of planting the bomb and of arms charges.
Dawson was sent to prison.

Despite Dawson's conviction, detectives knew that his imprisonment would not deter the TMS. They urged the public to be constantly on the lookout for anything suspicious...

NORTH AMERICA

The U.S. has recently experienced terrorist attacks within its borders, carried out by American terrorists and those from other countries. Several right-wing militias operate in the U.S. The Ku Klux Klan *(see page 6)* is trying to establish itself as a legitimate political party.

Devastation caused by the Oklahoma bomb.

MIDDLE EAST & AFRICA

The civil war in Lebanon (1975) and the revolution in Iran (1979) gave rise to several terrorist groups in the Middle East. Extreme Islamic terrorists such as Hizbollah (the Party of God) attack other religious groups in the region, as well as U.S. civilians and military. In Egypt, in 1981, the Muslim Brotherhood was responsible for the assassination of President Anwar Sadat.

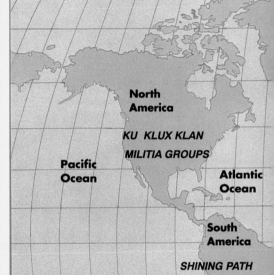

North America

KU KLUX KLAN
MILITIA GROUPS

Pacific
Ocean

Atlantic
Ocean

South
America

SHINING PATH

MONTONEROS

SOUTH AMERICA

In Peru, between 1980-1993, The Shining Path (Sendero Luminoso) killed 27,000 people and destroyed an estimated 23 billion dollars' worth of property in an attempt to shatter Peru's political structure.

In Argentina, the Montoneros continue to carry out terrorist attacks.

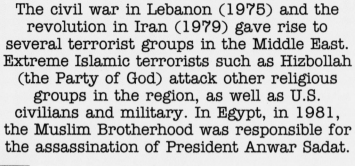

Sixty-one former members of the Shining Path surrender during a "ceremony" with the Peruvian president, Alberto Fujimori.

European countries, vulnerable to terrorist activity, operate border checks.

EUROPE & TURKEY

Two of the terrorist groups active in Northern Ireland are the mainly Catholic IRA *(see page 4)* and the mainly Protestant UVF (Ulster Volunteer Force). The IRA have carried out attacks both in Northern Ireland and on mainland Britain. In France, the imprisonment of four of the leaders of the anarchist movement Action Directe weakened the impact of the group whose aim is to bring down the French State. In Turkey, the Grey Wolves were allegedly involved in the attempted assassination of Pope John Paul II, in 1982. This organization was founded in 1976 to engage in operations against "enemies of the state."

Asia

GREY WOLVES

Europe

ETA
MAFIA   Turkey

Middle
East

MUSLIM BROTHERHOOD   **HIZBOLLAH**   **DAL KHALSA**

ISLAMIC JIHAD

Africa

TAMIL TIGERS

AUM SHINRIKYO

Pacific Ocean

PULO

Indian Ocean

Australia

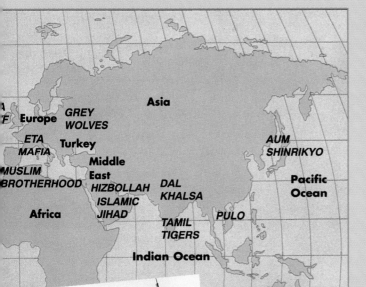

ASIA

In Japan, in 1994, the religious terrorist group Aum Shinrikyo (Supreme Truth) was allegedly responsible for releasing nerve gas on the Tokyo underground subway, killing 10 and injuring more than 5,500 people.
Kashmiri terrorists *(above left)* are fighting over the disputed territory of Kashmir for an independent state on the border of India and Pakistan.

The aftermath of a bomb planted by the Mafia *(see page 10)*, in Italy.

International Terrorism

Other major terrorist organizations across the world include:
India Dal Khalsa ● **Lebanon** Al Jihad al-Islami (Islamic Jihad) ● **Spain** ETA *(see page 11)* ● **Sri Lanka** People's Liberation Front & Liberation Tigers of Tamil (LTTE) ● **Thailand** Pattani United Liberation Organization (PULO)

GLOSSARY

Asylum Refuge given to a person, often by a country.

Cache Store of hidden goods.

Cordon A system of ribbons or blocks to seal off an area.

Detonators A device which ignites or sets off an explosive substance.

Extremist A person who holds extreme views.

Forensics Term relating to the use of clues and evidence in a court of law.

Hijacking Forcibly taking charge of a plane, train, or boat.

Hostages People who are held against their will by captors who will only release them when certain demands are met.

Informer A person who reports on the activities, illegal or not, of others.

Money laundering Making money from illegal activities look as if they come from legal businesses.

Racist A person who believes that his or her race is superior to anyone else's.

Suicide bombers People who carry bombs to their target, knowing they will die in the explosion.

INDEX